The Grandparent Book

by

Marcy Jackson

Dedicated to children
and grandparents
everywhere

RANDOM HOUSE
NEW YORK

Library of Congress Cataloging in Publication Data

Jackson, Marcy, 1952–
The grandparent book.

1. Grandparents.   2. Family.   I. Title.
HQ759.9.J33   1984   306.8'5   84-42740
ISBN 0-394-72755-X

Manufactured in the United States of America

24689753

This is a book for grandparents. We hope you will use it to make a permanent record for your grandchildren of what your own life has been like and of your recollections of those who came before you.

Many of us haven't thought about our childhood for years or, if we have, we've assumed such matters are of little interest to younger people. That isn't the case at all. We have a rich heritage to share. Our grandchildren, like the rest of us, long to understand their roots, yet they know almost nothing about those who came before them. Imagine the delight of a young girl who finds that her grandmother shared her love of poetry when she was growing up; or the excitement of a red-haired teenager on learning that his great-grandfather was known as "Red" Harrison. Even sad memories, or stories difficult to tell, can be very valuable for future generations.

Grandparents may live far away from their grandchildren so that it is difficult to communicate on a regular basis. In those circumstances, a written record can deepen their relationships.

This book is designed to be used by one grandparent. We hope the questions will help you cover all that you want to convey but there is also space at the end of the book to record other thoughts or to pass along information that is not covered in the questions.

As you sit down to write, try to let your thoughts flow through your pen. Don't worry about how elegant it sounds. What you're telling your family is much more important than the style of the writing. Try not to concentrate only on the good, wise, and happy things. Part of how we come to understand and make sense of our family background – and of ourselves – is by coming to terms with both the positive and the negative.

Finally, remember that whatever you share on these pages will be treasured by those who receive this gift. It could well be one of the most valuable inheritances you leave with your family.

ABOUT YOUR FAMILY...

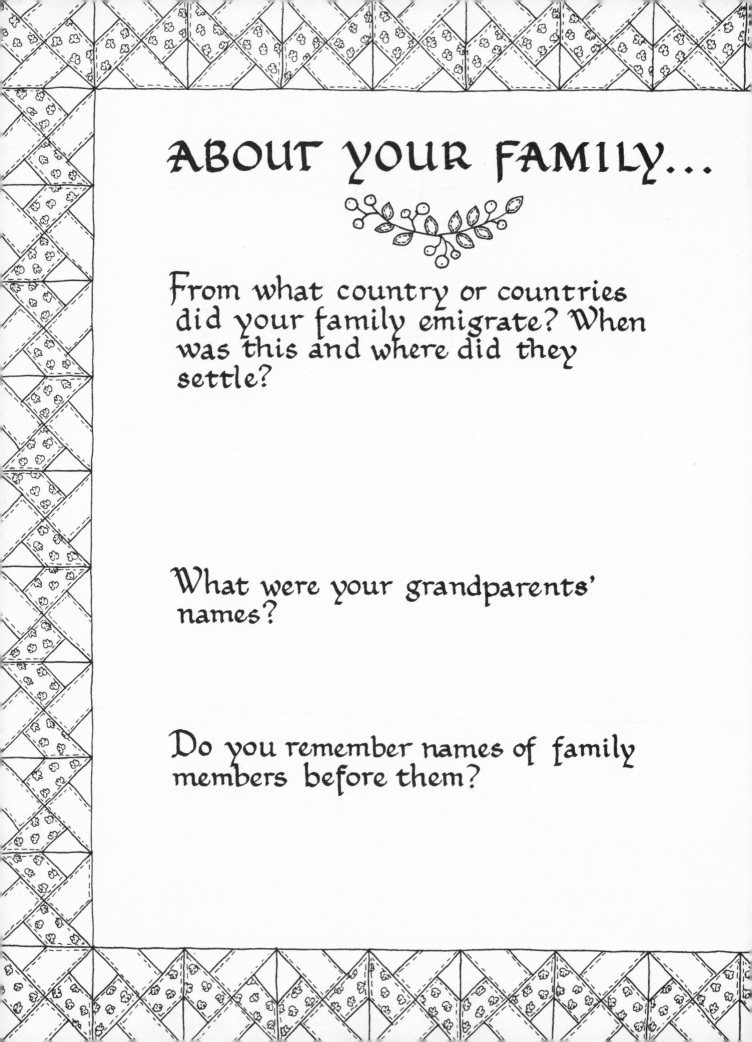

From what country or countries did your family emigrate? When was this and where did they settle?

What were your grandparents' names?

Do you remember names of family members before them?

What do you know about your grandparents' early years? Where did they grow up?

What do you remember about your grandparents or what stories have you heard about them?

Were there other relatives who were special to you or who played a role in your upbringing?

What are your parents' names?

When and where were they born?

What was your mother's maiden name?

What do you remember most about
your mother from your childhood?

What do you remember most about your father?

What special traits did you value most about your mother and father?

What work did your parents do?

What is your birthdate?

Where were you born?

Was there anything unusual about the circumstances of your birth?

Were you born in a hospital or at home?

What is your full name and how was it chosen? Does it have a special meaning?

Who in your family do you most look like?

How many brothers and sisters did you have? (List them in the order they were born and include children who may have died early in life or at birth)

Where did you fit among them?

To whom did you feel closest?

How did you spend your time together?

Did you ever take trips or vacations with your family? Where did you go? Tell about a favorite one.

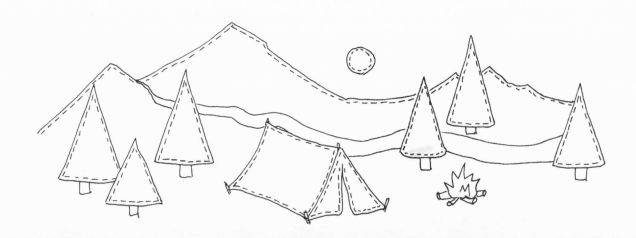

Was another language besides English spoken in your home? What was it?

Did your family attend a church or synagogue? Was religion an important part of your family life?

What were the family rules in your household?

Did your family have enough money? Was it ever a concern for you?

What were one or two of the worst
times in your family like?

What were one or two of the best
times like?

WHEN YOU WERE LITTLE....
(2-12 yrs.)

Where did you live? What do you remember most about your home(s)?

Describe what it was like where you grew up. How is that place different now?

Did you have any nicknames? What were they and did you like or dislike them?

Did you have any pets? Tell about them.

What did you do for fun? Describe your favorite toy or game.

What is your first memory going back as far as you can?

Were you ever really sick?

What do you remember about the grammar school you attended? How did you get there?

Did you have any favorite books or stories?

What did you want to be when you grew up?

What did your parents want you to do or be?

Do you remember how much things cost?

Clothes -

Food -

Movies -

Toys -

Gasoline -

Stamps -

WHEN YOU WERE GROWING UP (12 to 20 yrs.)....

What household chores or jobs did you have to do?

Did you get an allowance? How did you usually spend it?

What did you and your family use for transportation?

How many years of secondary school did you complete?

What parts of school did you like best? What parts did you like least?

Did you play any sports in school?

Were you involved in any music or drama activities? Tell about them.

Did you receive any awards or prizes for achievements in athletics, scholarship, etc.?

Were you a member of any clubs? What were they?

What songs and dances were popular?

What kind of clothing did you wear? How is it different than clothes worn by young people today?

Who most influenced your thinking during this time and why?

As a teenager, how did you get along with your parents?

At what point did you move away from home? Why and where did you go?

FAMILY TRADITIONS AND CELEBRATIONS...

Did you celebrate any special family or ethnic holidays at your house? Describe them.

As a child, how did you usually celebrate your birthday?

What was the best gift you ever got when you were young?

What was the best gift you ever gave?

Were there any traditional or favorite recipes that were usually prepared for family gatherings?

What religious holidays were celebrated in your home? Describe the family traditions associated with each, special foods served, favorite music and readings, etc.

What family or holiday traditions
have been the most meaningful to you?

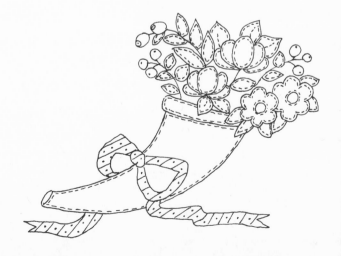

WHEN YOU GOT MARRIED...

1. How did you meet grandpa/grandma?

2. How old were you when you met?

3. What attracted you to each other?

What kinds of things did you like
to do together?

What do you remember most about
the courtship?

When did you decide to get married?
Describe the marriage proposal.

What did your parents say when you told them?

When and where was the wedding?

How old was each of you then?

What did you wear?

What do you remember most about your wedding day?

Who was there (in general)?

Did you go on a honeymoon? Tell about it.

What was your adjustment to married life like? Were there any surprises?

Where did you first live after you got married?

What stands out in your memory about your first year of marriage?

Tell a favorite story or two about grandpa/grandma.

Have you been married more than once? When and to whom?

How times were different then...

Entertainment –

Toys –

Chores or Cleaning –

Shopping –

Transportation -

Money/Economy -

Working -

Cooking -

Raising a family -

What do we have now that you
didn't have then?

What did you have then that we
don't have now?

BIG EVENTS IN YOUR LIFE..

What is the funniest thing that ever happened to you?

What was your proudest moment?

Most embarrassing moment?

Saddest or most painful time?

Where have you lived as an adult?
Where have you most enjoyed living
and why?

What was the biggest trip you have
ever taken as an adult? Where, when,
and with whom?

Did you ever serve in the military or become involved in wartime service? When and where?

What schools did you go to?

What kinds of courses did you take?

What honors or educational degrees have you earned?

Apart from school, what have been your most important learning experiences?

To what organizations have you belonged? (List only those that have been most important to you)

Have you ever been hospitalized? What for?

Are there any illnesses or medical conditions that seem to run in your family?

What was your first full-time job?
How much did you earn and what
responsibilities did you have?

What kinds of work have you done?

For pay -

Volunteer -

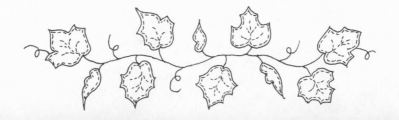

What have been your favorite hobbies or pastimes?

Do you have any collections (e.g. stamps, coins, rocks)?

Are there any family heirlooms that have been passed from one generation to another?

Have you ever met anyone famous?

What major inventions have been developed in your lifetime?

What scientific or medical discovery in your lifetime has impressed you most?

Have you been actively involved in politics, either as a candidate or campaign supporter?

As you look back do you have any favorite years? What made them so special?

Is there a time in your life you would like to live over?

YOUR VIEWS AND FEELINGS...

What are some of the best books you have ever read?

What is one of your favorite sayings?

What do you think is special or unique about our family?

What do you most value in a friend?

Who are or were your closest friends?
How long have you known them and
what makes them so special?

In times of trouble who or what has
helped pull you through?

What issues or causes have you felt strongly about?

What values or religious beliefs do you hold dear?

What major happenings in the world have affected your life most?

What are your feelings about the world today? What concerns you most?

What are your views of our political system?

What's your best advice for your grandchildren?

What are your hopes and dreams for the future?

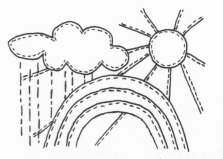

ABOUT YOUR CHILDREN...

1. What are your children's names and when were they born?

2. How did you choose their names? Have any of them been passed down through the family?

What are some of your favorite recollections of your family life when your children were young?

How were your children different
from each other when they were little?

In what ways did you raise your children
like your parents raised you?

In what ways did you raise them differently?

What parts of being a parent have been most difficult or trying for you?

What parts were easiest or most rewarding?

How did you find out that you'd become a grandparent for the first time? How did you feel?

By what names have you been called by your grandchildren?

What have you liked most about being a grandparent?

What are your wishes for your grandchildren?

ADDITIONAL THOUGHTS

MEMORABILIA
(Letters, Photographs, etc.)